MACMILLAN R[
INTERMEDIATE

DAPHNE DU MAURIER

My Cousin Rachel

Retold by Margaret Tarner

INTERMEDIATE LEVEL

Founding Editor: John Milne

The Macmillan Readers provide a choice of enjoyable reading materials for learners of English. The series is published at six levels – Starter, Beginner, Elementary, Pre-intermediate, Intermediate and Upper.

Level control
Information, structure and vocabulary are controlled to suit the students' ability at each level.

The number of words at each level:

Starter	about 300 basic words
Beginner	about 600 basic words
Elementary	about 1100 basic words
Pre-intermediate	about 1400 basic words
Intermediate	about 1600 basic words
Upper	about 2200 basic words

Vocabulary
Some difficult words and phrases in this book are important for understanding the story. Some of these words are explained in the story and some are shown in the pictures. From Pre-intermediate level upwards, words are marked with a number like this: ...³. These words are explained in the Glossary at the end of the book.

Contents

1

I Begin My Story

My father and mother died before I was two years old. I cannot remember them. My father died first, fighting in the war against the French in 1815. My mother died a few months afterwards. My cousin Ambrose, who was twenty years older than me, became my guardian[1]. He looked after me as if I was his son. From the beginning, I loved Ambrose more than anyone else in the world.

Ambrose Ashley was a rich, unmarried man. He lived in a beautiful old house in the west of England. The house was near the sea and there was farmland all round it. The house, the land and the farms around it had all belonged to the Ashley family for many years. The house was full of pictures, books and many beautiful things.

Ambrose was a gentleman of leisure[2]. He was not a business-man. But he took good care of all the people who worked on his land. He knew them all by name. Everyone on the estate[3] loved Ambrose as much as I did.

Ambrose was a shy[4] man, with many unusual ideas. He looked after me himself and would not have a woman in the house to help him. But he was friendly with the people who lived in the other big houses in the district[5]. Some of his neighbours did not understand Ambrose, but they all liked him.

As I grew older, Ambrose and I became more like brothers. We were both tall, shy men, with long arms and legs and big feet. We both had thick, curly hair, although Ambrose's hair was darker than mine.

We enjoyed doing the same things. We often rode our horses through the beautiful woods and fields near the house. When the weather was good, we sailed our boat on the sea, fished, or swam.

There were no female servants in the Ashley house. Ambrose said he did not want women in the house.

And as I grew older, I agreed more and more with his ideas. The big house was not very clean or tidy, but it was comfortable and we both loved it. The servants looked after us well and the food and wine were always good. Ambrose and I often sat together after dinner, drinking wine in the light of our candles. Then we sat in the library beside a bright fire. The walls of the library were covered with shelves full of beautiful books.

On Sundays, we always went to church. After breakfast, the carriage took Ambrose and me to the church in the village. All the servants came to church too. On Sunday evenings, we had an early dinner. Usually, some of our neighbours would eat with us.

When I was old enough, Ambrose taught me how to look after his land and his people. I was his heir. The house and the land were going to be mine when Ambrose died. But I never thought that Ambrose would die. We both expected[6] that he would live for many years. Our days together passed in a calm happiness.

But sometimes changes come into people's lives that they do

not expect. Things happen to us that we can do nothing about. My dear cousin Ambrose is dead. That is why I am writing this story. My cousin Rachel is dead too. And who was my cousin Rachel? You must read my story to find the answer to that question.

I know who killed Rachel, but I do not know how my dear Ambrose died. Was he killed too? I shall never be able to answer that question. I shall never know the answer. Perhaps, you who are reading this can decide. You must be my cousin Rachel's judge[7] and mine too.

I, Philip Ashley, am only twenty-five now. Most of my life is in front of me. But the only people I shall ever love are dead. I cannot live with my thoughts any longer. I must write down everything that happened – everything about Ambrose, my cousin Rachel and myself.

2

News From Italy

Ambrose and I lived in Cornwall. It is often cold and damp in winter there. Rain falls nearly every day and the sea looks rough and grey. This weather was bad for Ambrose. By the time he was forty years old, he was walking with a stick and his hair was turning grey. His doctors told him that he must go abroad every winter to a drier country. If he did this, he would become stronger and he would live to be a healthy, old man.

I was twenty-two when Ambrose went abroad for the third winter. I had left University and I was old enough to look after the estate by myself.

This time, Ambrose was going to Italy. He wanted to see the beautiful gardens of Rome and Florence. Ambrose loved his own gardens and everything he planted grew well there. Now he was planning to bring back many unusual plants and trees from Italy.

The evening before Ambrose left for Italy, we sat together in the library as usual. We were both smoking our pipes and our long legs were stretched out in front of us. We were wearing old, comfortable clothes and the fire was burning brightly. The dogs were sleeping at our feet. We sat in silence for a while and then Ambrose said, 'I wish you were coming with me tomorrow, Philip.'

'Why not?' I replied quickly. 'I could soon be ready. Yes, Ambrose, let me go with you.'

Ambrose smiled. 'No,' he said. 'We can't both be away. Someone must look after the estate. Forget I asked you.'

'You are feeling well, aren't you?' I asked. 'You haven't any pain?'

'Of course not, Philip,' Ambrose replied. 'The trouble is that I love my home too much. I don't want to leave.'

Ambrose stood up and walked towards the windows. He pulled back the heavy curtains and looked out into the darkness.

'You must promise to look after the gardens for me, Philip,' he said.

'What do you mean?' I asked. 'You will be back here in the spring.'

'Yes, I will . . .' Ambrose answered slowly. 'Take care of things while I'm away, Philip. You are very young, but I need your help, you know that. And everything I have will be yours.'

Suddenly I felt afraid.

'Ambrose, please let me go to Italy with you,' I said again.

'No, Philip, that's enough,' Ambrose said with a smile. 'Go to bed.' That was all. We did not discuss the matter again.

Early the following morning, Ambrose left for Plymouth, our nearest big port. He was going by ship to the south of France. From there, he would travel by coach[8] to Italy.

———

The weeks passed slowly for me. They always did when Ambrose was away. But I had plenty to do. And if I was lonely, I rode my horse into the nearest town or visited our neighbours.

The first letter from Ambrose arrived in the middle of November. He was well and happy. The journey by ship had gone well. At Christmas, Ambrose wrote to say that he had reached Florence. It was in this letter that he wrote about his cousin Rachel for the first time. He told me that our family and her family were related. Rachel's father and mother were both dead. Rachel's husband, an Italian count, had died too. She lived alone near Florence in a big house, called the Villa Sangalletti. Rachel had planted the gardens of the villa herself and they were famous for their beauty.

I was glad when I read this letter. Ambrose had found a friend who loved gardens as much as he did.

The winter in Europe was very bad that year and snow covered the roads. Because of this, the next letter did not arrive until the early spring. In this letter, Ambrose told me more about his cousin Rachel. She had found him somewhere to stay near her villa.

My cousin Rachel is a very intelligent woman, Ambrose wrote. *But, thank God, she doesn't talk too much. Her gardens are beautiful. The weather is getting warmer and I am spending a lot of time in them. My cousin Rachel is pleased to have an English friend and I am giving her advice about business matters. She has very little money. Because I have helped her, my cousin Rachel has helped me find many beautiful plants. I will bring them home with me.*

I was surprised by this letter. Ambrose had never shown any

interest in a woman before. But I was glad that he was well and happy.

There were a few more letters, but Ambrose did not say anything about returning to Cornwall. Then at the end of April, I received the letter that changed my whole life.

Dear boy,

I don't know how to begin to tell you – my cousin Rachel and I were married two weeks ago. I do not know why she has chosen me. But we are very happy together. I love her, Philip, and I am sure you will love her too. She is kind and good.

Tell our friends about my marriage, Philip. And remember, it will never change my feelings for you. Write soon and send some words of welcome to your cousin Rachel.

I could not believe it. I took the letter out in the gardens and walked slowly down to the sea. I sat there and read the letter again. I felt lonely, angry and very unhappy. I was already jealous[9] of this woman, my cousin Rachel. I knew that my life would never be the same again.

I told all the neighbours about Ambrose's marriage. But I did not speak to anyone about my feelings. To my surprise, all our neighbours were very happy at the news. 'It's the best thing that could have happened. When are they coming home?' people said. But I did not know. Ambrose had not written anything about when he would come back.

Our nearest friends were Nick Kendall and his daughter, Louise. Nick Kendall was nearly sixty years old. He was my godfather[10]. His wife was dead. Louise was a little younger than me and people said she was pretty. We had known each other all our lives and she was like a sister to me. The Kendalls were the first people I told about Ambrose's marriage.

Nick Kendall was a lawyer. When he heard the news, he looked at me carefully.

'You will have to start looking for a house, Philip,' he said.

At first I did not understand.

'What do you mean?' I asked in surprise.

'Well, Ambrose and his wife will want to be together,' Nick Kendall told me. 'They may have children. I am sure Ambrose will buy you a house of your own. And you may get married yourself. There are many pretty girls in the district.'

He went on talking, but I did not hear what he said. I had never thought I would have to leave my home. I hated my cousin Rachel. What was she like, this woman who was completely changing my life? Was she pretty or plain, old or young?

In the middle of May, I received another letter from Ambrose. He said that he and my cousin Rachel were staying in Italy for the summer. I was so happy. Thank God, this woman was not going to come to the house yet! I began to enjoy life again.

The summer passed and winter came. Ambrose did not return. He continued to write to me but his letters changed. I began to feel that he was not happy. The summer and autumn were very hot in Italy that year. Ambrose was having terrible headaches. He had never had headaches before. But he said nothing about coming home.

The second winter passed and then the spring. Ambrose had been married for more than a year now. Many weeks passed and I did not receive a letter. I began to worry. At last a letter came in July. But it made me more worried than before. I got on my horse at once and rode over to Nick Kendall's house to show him the letter.

The writing was so bad that we could hardly read it. Ambrose wrote to say that he had a terrible illness. He wrote about his fear of Italian doctors and of a man called Rainaldi. He also seemed to be afraid of his wife, Rachel.

'These are the words of a very sick man,' Nick Kendall said slowly. 'A man whose mind is very disturbed[11]. You do not know this, Philip, but Ambrose's father died of a tumour[12] of the brain. In the last weeks of his life, he was sometimes like a madman. I hope that Ambrose . . .'

Then Nick Kendall looked at me and said, 'I think you had better go to Italy, Philip. You must find out what is happening.'

I knew immediately that I had to go to Italy. I did not look forward to the long journey in a strange country. I could not speak French or Italian. But I knew I had to go.

I went home and got ready to leave. Seecombe, our head servant, was going to look after the house while I was away. I did not tell him about Ambrose's illness.

I was in the carriage ready to leave when a last letter arrived from Ambrose. It was very short and almost impossible to read.

For God's sake, come quickly! Ambrose had written. *Rachel, my torment[13], has won. I am dying. Come quickly, or it will be too late!*

I began my journey with a terrible fear in my heart. It was the 10th of July. I knew I could not reach Ambrose until the middle of August.

3

The Villa Sangalletti

I had a terrible journey. The roads were noisy and dirty. The weather got hotter every day. By the time I reached Florence, it was the 15th of August.

I found a room in a hotel and washed and changed my clothes. When I went out again, the streets were full of people. It was about four o'clock in the afternoon and still very hot. I stopped a carriage.

'Villa Sangalletti,' I said to the driver. He nodded and pointed up the hill.

The horse pulled the carriage slowly up a long, twisting road. At last, the driver stopped in front of a gate in a high wall. I made signs to him to wait.

There was a bell beside the gate and I pulled it hard. I waited a few moments, but no one came. I rang the bell again. I heard the sounds of a dog barking and a child crying. It was very hot. Then I heard footsteps and the gate slowly opened. A servant woman stood in the gateway. There was a long, wide path behind her. It led to the villa.

'Villa Sangalletti? Signor Ashley?' I asked.

The woman tried to shut the gate, but I pushed past her. A man appeared and the woman shouted to him in Italian. I heard the words: 'Ashley . . . Inglese . . .'

The man stared at me. 'I speak a little English, signore,' he said. 'Can I help you?'

'I have come here to see Mr Ashley,' I said. 'Are Mr and Mrs Ashley at the villa?'

The man looked worried.

'Are you Signor Ashley's son, signore?' he asked.

'No,' I said, 'I am his cousin. Tell me quickly. Is he at home?'

'You are from England, signore?' the man asked slowly. 'You have not heard the news? Signor Ashley, he died three weeks ago. Very sudden. After the funeral[14], the contessa, his wife, shut up the villa and went away. We do not know if she will come back again.'

I did not say anything. There was nothing I could say.

'Signor,' the man said kindly, 'I will open the villa for you. You can see where Signor Ashley died.'

I was not interested in where I went or what I did. The man began to walk up the path, taking some keys from his pocket. I followed.

The villa was very beautiful. All the windows were closed and shuttered[15]. The man opened the big door. He and the woman began to open the shutters. The rooms were large and the air was dry and dusty.

'The Villa Sangalletti is beautiful, signore, very old,' said the man. 'The Signor Ashley, this is where he sat. This was his chair.'

I looked at the chair. I could not think of Ambrose in this house, in this room.

I went to the window. Outside, there was a little courtyard[16]. It was open to the sky, but shaded from the sun. In the middle of the courtyard, there was a fountain[17] and a little pool. A laburnum tree[18] stood beside the pool. Its golden flowers had died. And its small, green seeds lay on the ground.

'Signor Ashley, he sat here every day,' the man said. 'He liked to listen to the water falling. He sat there, under the tree. In summer, they always sat here, Signor Ashley and the contessa. They drank their tisana[19] here, after dinner. Day after day, always the same.'

It was very cool there in the courtyard and very, very quiet. I thought of how Ambrose had lived at home – walking, riding, always cheerful and busy.

'I will show you the room where Signor Ashley died,' the man said quietly. I followed him upstairs into the plain, bare room.

Outside, there was a little courtyard.

I looked at the small, hard bed where Ambrose had died.

'He died suddenly,' the man told me. 'He was very weak from the fever. But sometimes he shouts, like a madman. Then one morning, the contessa called for me.

'He was lying very still. It was the sleep of death. He had a peaceful face. The pain and the madness had all gone.'

'Madness? What do you mean?' I said.

'The madness of the fever,' the man replied. 'He suffered much pain. Sometimes, I had to hold him down in his bed. Then came the fever and the madness. I tell you, signore, it was terrible to see.'

I turned away.

'Why was nothing done?' I said. 'Why did Mrs Ashley let him die? What was this illness? How long did it last?'

'At the end, it was very sudden, like I told you,' said the man. 'But he had been very ill all winter. And he was sad. All winter he was sad.'

We walked through another room and out onto a long terrace[20]. In front of us were the most beautiful gardens I had ever seen.

'I think,' the man said slowly, 'that the contessa will not come back again. Too sad for her. Signor Rainaldi told us that perhaps the villa will be sold.'

'Who is Signor Rainaldi?' I asked quickly.

'He arranges things for the contessa,' the man replied. 'Money, business, everything. I give you his address. He speaks English very well.'

He closed the shutters. We walked downstairs again and stood by the big door.

'What happened to his clothes?' I asked. 'Where are his books, his papers?'

'The contessa took everything with her.'

'And you don't know where she went?' I asked.

The man shook his head.

'She has left Florence. That is all I know. Signor Ashley was buried here in Florence, signore, then the contessa left.'

The woman suddenly spoke to her husband and opened a chest[21] near the wall. She came back carrying a big straw hat – Ambrose's hat. The hat that he had sometimes worn at home, in the sun. The woman gave it to me and I stood there with it in my hands.

'Take it with you, signore,' the man said softly. 'It is yours now.'

4

I Meet Rainaldi

On my journey back to Florence, I thought of only one thing. I had to speak to Signor Rainaldi. He must know more about Ambrose's death.

The servant at the villa had given me Signor Rainaldi's address. I found the house at last, in a quiet, dark street. Signor Rainaldi was at home and a servant took me to his room.

Rainaldi looked surprised when he saw me. He was a thin man, about forty years old, with a proud, hard face.

'My name is Ashley – Philip Ashley,' I said.

'Yes,' Signor Rainaldi answered. 'Will you sit down? You are Ambrose Ashley's cousin – and his heir. You look very like him. I did not expect to see you here. When did you arrive in Florence?'

'This afternoon,' I replied. 'I have been to the Villa Sangalletti.'

Signor Rainaldi smiled. 'Then you have not seen your cousin Rachel,' he said. 'She left Florence very suddenly. Your cousin's death was a great shock to her.'

'It was a shock to me, too, Signor Rainaldi,' I said. 'Why

wasn't I told about Ambrose's illness?'

'Mrs Ashley always hoped he would get well,' Rainaldi answered. 'She did not want to worry you.'

'But I had these letters,' I said. 'That is why I came to Florence.' And I handed Rainaldi the last two letters from Ambrose. When he had read them Signor Rainaldi said slowly, 'Yes, the doctors warned[22] Mrs Ashley of this.'

'What do you mean?'

'They told her that your cousin had a tumour on his brain. That is why he wrote these letters. First the tumour destroyed[23] his brain and then it killed him.'

I shook my head. I could not believe it.

Rainaldi held out a paper. 'This is a copy of the death certificate[24],' he said. 'I sent another copy of it to you in Cornwall and one to Mr Kendall. As your guardian, he had to be told about Ambrose's death.'

'Mr Kendall is my guardian?' I asked in surprise. 'Ambrose never told me that.'

'It is in your cousin's will[25],' Rainaldi replied. 'Mr Kendall will explain when you return home.'

'But what about these letters?' I cried. 'Ambrose wrote them to warn me. He was not sick, but in great danger.'

'Your Cousin Ambrose was sick in his mind,' Rainaldi answered. 'His sickness gave him strange ideas. Because Mrs Ashley was with him all the time, he suspected[26] her. A sick man often thinks that his dearest friends are his enemies.'

'If I had been here, Ambrose would be alive now,' I said.

Rainaldi shook his head. 'No,' he said. 'That is not true. No one could do anything for him.'

I turned and moved towards the door.

'When Mrs Ashley returns, tell her I know about the letters,' I said.

'Your cousin Rachel left Florence very suddenly,' Rainaldi said. 'I do not think she will come back.'

I walked out of the cold house and into the dark streets. I did not believe Rainaldi's story. Ambrose had died in great pain and unhappiness. And my cousin Rachel had been the cause of his pain. I was sure of that.

I promised myself that one day I would bring pain and unhappiness to my cousin Rachel. I would punish this woman who had killed my dear Ambrose, far away from his home and his friends.

5

An Argument and an Arrival

I arrived home in the first week of September. I had sent letters and the servants were already dressed in black[27]. My journey to Italy seemed like a dream.

I was glad to be home. I was responsible now for the house and estate. I had to look after them as Ambrose had done. I wanted to do my work well.

My godfather, Nick Kendall, visited me as soon as I got back.

He brought his daughter, Louise, with him. Nick Kendall had come to explain Ambrose's will to me.

'The house and the estate will be yours when you are twenty-five, Philip,' he told me. 'But for the next seven months, I am your guardian. If you want money, you must come to me. Of course, I hope, one day, you will marry. This place needs a woman, Philip.'

'I want no woman,' I said. 'Ambrose married, and it killed him.

'My cousin Rachel left Florence the day after the funeral,' I went on. 'Signor Rainaldi told me. She took all Ambrose's things with her, like a thief.'

'You must not call your cousin's wife a thief,' Nick Kendall said. 'If Ambrose had changed his will when he married, everything would now belong to her. I am surprised that your cousin Rachel has not made a claim[28].'

'A claim!' I cried. 'But she was the cause of Ambrose's death!'

'Nonsense, Philip,' said Nick Kendall. 'Ambrose died of a brain tumour. That is why he wrote those terrible letters.'

'I don't believe it,' I said.

'You don't want to believe it,' my godfather replied angrily. 'Keep those ideas to yourself, Philip. If you don't, there will be trouble.'

I said nothing.

I did not see the Kendalls again for nearly two weeks. Then Nick Kendall asked me to go and see him. I found him in his study[29], a letter in his hand.

'Well,' he said slowly, 'I have news for you, Philip. This is a letter from your cousin Rachel. She has come to England with Ambrose's things. She asks for nothing. She only wants to see the house that Ambrose lived in. She is in a strange country, without a friend. You ought to see her, Philip.'

I smiled.

20

'Of course I'll see my cousin Rachel,' I said in a hard, cold voice. 'I want to see her very much. Tell her that when you write to her. Tell her that Philip Ashley invites his cousin Rachel to his home.'

Nick Kendall understood my feelings. 'You have become very hard, Philip,' he said. 'I hope you will not say anything stupid when Mrs Ashley is here. She was your cousin's wife. You must remember that.'

I went out into the garden and saw Louise walking there. When I told her about my cousin Rachel's visit, she was very surprised. 'No woman has stayed in that house for twenty years,' Louise said. 'Think how dusty and untidy it is!'

'It was good enough for Ambrose,' I said. 'She won't think about the house when I begin to question her! She'll cry – and I'll be pleased!'

But when I got home, I changed my mind[30]. I wanted to show my cousin Rachel that I was a gentleman. I wanted her to know that I was a man who looked after his property. I spoke to the head servant, Seecombe. He agreed that the whole house must be cleaned before Mrs Ashley arrived.

'We must make Mrs Ashley welcome,' Seecombe said. 'Shall I prepare Mr Ambrose's room for her?'

'Certainly not,' I said. 'I am moving into Mr Ashley's room. Get the blue room ready for Mrs Ashley.'

On the day my cousin Rachel arrived, the house looked completely different. Everything was clean and tidy. Seecombe had got out all the silver[31] and cleaned it. Tamlyn, the head gardener, had filled every room with flowers.

I looked around the house and then walked up slowly to the blue room. The dogs followed me. The rooms for my cousin Rachel were clean. The windows were wide open.

There was a portrait[32] of Ambrose on one wall. It had been painted when he was a young man. He had looked very much like me. I smiled at the portrait and felt a little happier.

My cousin Rachel was going to arrive some time in the afternoon. I decided that I did not want to be in the house when she arrived. Although the day was cold and windy, I went out alone after lunch. I walked until I was tired. I did not return until after six o'clock.

There was a fire in the library, but the room was empty. I pulled the bell and rang for Seecombe.

'Madam has come,' Seecombe said. 'She is tired and is having some food in her room. She will be pleased to see you after dinner.'

'Where is her luggage?' I asked Seecombe.

'Madam has very little luggage of her own,' answered Seecombe. 'It has been taken upstairs to her room. All of Mr Ambrose's boxes have arrived with her. We have put them in your room, as she asked.'

So I had my dinner alone and drank a glass of brandy. Then I went upstairs and knocked at the door of my cousin Rachel's sitting-room.

A quiet voice answered my knock.

6

Tea With My Cousin

I went into the room. Everything was neat and tidy. The candles had been lit, but the curtains were still open. The dogs were in front of the fire. A woman was sitting with her back to the door.

'Good evening,' I said.

She turned at once, got up and walked towards me. Now at last, I was face to face with my cousin Rachel. She was a small woman, dressed completely in black. Her dark hair was very neat. As she looked at me, her large, dark eyes opened wide in surprise.

'I hope you are rested,' I said awkwardly[33].

'Thank you, Philip, yes.' She sat down by the fire and the old dog, Don, laid his head on her knee.

'Don is your dog, isn't he?' she said. 'Is it true that he is almost fifteen?'

'Yes,' I said. 'Ambrose gave him to me on my tenth birthday.'

'I know,' she answered softly. Then my cousin Rachel stood up and moved towards the window.

'I want to thank you, Philip, for letting me come,' she said. 'It can't have been easy for you.'

It had started to rain. She closed the curtains and we both sat down again.

'I felt so strange, driving up to the house,' my cousin Rachel said. 'Ambrose told me so much about it. I was longing[34] to be h . . . here.'

She hesitated[35] on the last word. I knew she had nearly said 'home'.

'I hope you will be comfortable here,' I said. 'There are no women servants in the house to look after you.'

'That doesn't matter. I don't need anyone to look after me. I have only two dresses, and some strong shoes for walking.'

'Now at last, I was face to face with my cousin Rachel.'

She smiled and I smiled back. Then I suddenly felt angry. Why was I smiling at this woman who had caused my dear Ambrose's death?

At that moment, Seecombe came into the room.

'Tea[36] is served, madam,' Seecombe said, putting down the large silver tray. On the tray was a large silver teapot that I had never seen before.

'What about breakfast, madam?' Seecombe went on. 'Mr Philip has his at eight o'clock.'

'I would like mine in my room,' my cousin Rachel answered. 'Would that be too much trouble?'

'Certainly not, madam. Come dogs – downstairs. Goodnight madam, goodnight, sir.'

My cousin Rachel poured me some tea. Seecombe had never served tea after dinner before, but I said nothing.

'If you want to smoke your pipe, you can, Philip,' my cousin Rachel said.

I stared at her. I did not expect to smoke in a lady's room. I had wanted to say a few hard[37] words and then leave. Now here I was, drinking tea and smoking my pipe. But how could I be angry with this small, neat woman – or hate her?

The next thing I heard was a quiet voice saying, 'You're nearly asleep, Philip. Hadn't you better go to bed? You walked a long way today, didn't you?'

I opened my eyes and moved my long legs. Was my cousin Rachel laughing at me? Did she know why I had stayed away from the house all afternoon?

I got up slowly and looked down at her.

'Wait a minute, Philip,' my cousin Rachel said. 'I have a present for you.'

She went into her bedroom and came out with a stick – Ambrose's walking stick. It was the one he had always used. I took it awkwardly.

'Now go!' she said. 'Please go quickly. You remind[38] me so much of Ambrose . . .'

I stood outside the door for a moment, holding the stick in my hands. Had this woman really killed Ambrose? I had seen the look of deep unhappiness on her face. Already, my ideas about her were changing.

7

A Strange Conversation

The following day was Saturday. I paid the men their wages, as Ambrose had always done. But Tamlyn, the head gardener, was not there. I was told that he was in the gardens somewhere, with the mistress.

I found them putting new plants into the ground.

'I've been here since half past ten,' my cousin Rachel said with a smile. 'These are some of the plants Ambrose and I found in Italy. I had to put them into the ground quickly. Tamlyn has been helping me.'

'And I've learnt a lot of things this morning, Mr Philip,' Tamlyn said. 'Mrs Ashley knows far more about these plants than I do.'

After lunch, I took my cousin Rachel around the estate. She sat on a quiet horse and I walked beside her. She wore a black dress and a black shawl[39] round her head. She looked very proud and very Italian – not like an Englishwoman at all.

To my surprise, my cousin Rachel knew the name of every field and farm on the estate. As I walked by her side, we began to talk about the gardens of my cousin Rachel's villa.

'When I was married to my first husband,' she said, 'I was

not happy. So I spent my time planning the gardens of the Villa Sangalletti. I would like you to see them, Philip.'

I looked up in surprise. Didn't my cousin Rachel know that I had been to Florence and seen the villa? I thought my godfather had told her in his letter. I began to speak, but the horse moved on and it was too late. I was very quiet on the way home.

After dinner, we sat down together by the library fire. My cousin Rachel was sewing[40]. I smoked my pipe and watched her hands moving quickly. They were small, white hands and she wore two rings on her fingers.

'Something is the matter, Philip,' she said at last. 'What is worrying you?'

'Did my godfather tell you I had been away?'

'No.'

'I didn't hear of Ambrose's death from Signor Rainaldi's letter,' I said slowly. 'I found out about it in Florence, from your servants.'

My cousin Rachel gave me a long, strange look.

'You went to Florence?' she said. 'When? For how long?'

'I was in Florence for only one night – the night of the 15th of August,' I said.

The sewing fell from my cousin Rachel's hands.

'But I left Florence only the day before. Why didn't you tell me this last night?'

'I thought you knew,' I answered awkwardly.

'I want you to tell me why you went to Italy, Philip,' my cousin Rachel said.

I put my hand in my pocket and felt the letters there.

'I had not heard from Ambrose for a long time,' I said. 'As the weeks went by, I grew worried. Then in July, a letter came, a very strange letter. I showed it to Nick Kendall. He agreed that I should go to Florence at once. As I was leaving, there was another letter. I have them both in my pocket. Do you want to see them?'

'Not yet. Tell me what you did in Florence.'

'I went to the Villa Sangalletti. When I asked for Ambrose, the servants told me he was dead. You had gone away. They showed me the room where Ambrose had died and gave me his hat. It was the only thing you had left behind.'

My cousin Rachel sat very still.

'Go on,' she said quietly.

'I went back to Florence, to Signor Rainaldi. He told me about Ambrose's illness. He did not know where you were. I left for England the following day.'

There was silence and then my cousin Rachel said, 'May I see the letters now?'

She read them over and over again. At last, she handed them back.

Then my cousin Rachel looked deep into my eyes.

'How you must have hated me, Philip,' she said.

At that moment, I felt that my cousin Rachel knew everything. She knew everything I had been thinking about her, all these months.

'Yes, I have hated you,' I said slowly.

'Then why did you ask me here?'

'To accuse[41] you of breaking his heart, perhaps – a kind of murder. I wanted to make you suffer, to watch you suffer.'

'You have your wish,' she said. Her face was very white and her dark eyes were full of tears.

I stood up and looked away. I had never seen a woman cry before.

'Cousin Rachel, go upstairs,' I said. But she did not move. I took the letters from her hands and threw them in the fire.

'I can forget,' I said, 'if you will too. Look, the letters have burnt away.'

'We can both remember what Ambrose wrote,' my cousin Rachel replied. 'But it's better if I say nothing more. I cannot explain. Let me stay until Monday. Then I will go away. Then you can either forget me, or go on hating me. At least we were happy today, Philip.'

'But I do not hate you now,' I said. 'I hated someone I had never met. Even before those letters came, I hated Ambrose's wife because I was jealous. Ambrose is the only person I have ever loved. You took him away from me and I was jealous of you. Love can do strange things to people.'

'I know that,' my cousin Rachel answered. 'Love did strange things to Ambrose too. He was forty-three when we met and he fell in love. He was like someone who had been asleep all his life. His love was too strong. It was too strong for me and too strong for him. It changed him, Philip.'

'What do you mean?' I asked.

'Something in me made Ambrose change,' she replied. 'Sometimes I made him happy, sometimes I made him sad. Then he became ill. You were right to hate me, Philip. If Ambrose hadn't met me he would be alive today.'

She looked at me and smiled sadly.

'Perhaps I was jealous of you too, Philip,' she said. 'He was always talking about you. Sometimes I grew very tired of hearing your name.'

She stopped talking and picked up her sewing. 'If you wish, we can talk again tomorrow,' my cousin Rachel said. 'Then, on Monday, I shall leave. Nick Kendall has invited me to stay in his house.'

'But I don't want you to go,' I said. 'There are so many things to do together . . .'

As I looked down at her, her eyes seemed to see through me and understand all my thoughts.

'Light me a candle,' she said. 'I must go to bed.'

Then she stood above me on the stairs, looking down at me.

'You don't hate me any more?' she asked.

'No. And are you still jealous of me, or is that forgotten too?'

My cousin Rachel laughed. 'I was never jealous of you,' she said. 'I was jealous of a spoilt[42] boy whom I had never met.'

Suddenly she bent down and kissed me.

'Your first kiss, Philip,' she said. 'I hope you like it.'

I watched her as she walked up the stairs, away from me.

8

Two Letters

On Sundays, Ambrose and I had always gone to church. This Sunday, my cousin Rachel agreed to go with me. Our neighbours were able to see her for the first time and the church was full. I heard people saying that my cousin Rachel was beautiful. This surprised me very much.

As usual, the Kendalls and the vicar and his family came to dinner. I had never enjoyed these visits. But, to my surprise, the afternoon was a great success. The time passed quickly. How I wished Ambrose had been with us! Everyone enjoyed themselves, except, I think, Louise. She said very little and did not smile once.

When our guests left at six o'clock, my cousin Rachel and I went back into the library.

'Well, Philip,' my cousin Rachel asked me, 'have you enjoyed yourself?'

'Yes, but I don't know why,' I answered. 'Everyone seemed more interesting than usual.'

'When you marry Louise, it will always be like that,' my cousin Rachel said with a smile. 'A man needs a wife when he is entertaining[43].'

I stared at her.

'Marry Louise?' I repeated in surprise. 'I am not going to marry Louise, or anyone.'

'Aren't you?' my cousin Rachel replied. 'Your godfather thinks you are. And Louise does too. She will make you a good wife. When I am gone, you will need a woman here.'

'But you are not going, cousin Rachel,' I told her. 'What is wrong with this house and with me?'

'Nothing . . .'

'Tomorrow, you must begin visiting,' I went on. 'Then our neighbours will visit you. You will have many things to do here.'

'I don't think I really like that idea,' said my cousin Rachel, standing up. 'It would be better if I gave your neighbours Italian lessons. I am a poor widow[44] and shall need money soon.'

I laughed. 'Then you must marry or sell your rings!'

I knew at once that I had been very rude. It was true that my cousin Rachel had nothing. She could not live without money.

I called the dog and went out into the garden. I felt very stupid and I stayed away from the house until it was dark. As I was walking, I had an idea. Some money must be given to my cousin Rachel. But I would not tell her that it was my idea.

When I turned back to the house, I saw that the windows of Rachel's bedroom were open.

'Why are you walking in the dark, Philip?' a soft voice asked. 'Are you worried about anything?'

'Why, yes,' I answered. 'I'm afraid you must find me very rude and stupid.'

'Nonsense, Philip. Go to bed.'

Something fell at my feet. It was a flower. The window was closed quietly.

———

That week, more plants and small trees arrived from Italy. On Thursday morning, I rode over to Pelyn, my godfather's house. My cousin Rachel was in the garden with Tamlyn. She told me that she and the gardeners would be busy until the afternoon.

I wasted no time and I was in my godfather's study by ten o'clock.

'My cousin Rachel must have some money,' I said. 'She is talking about giving Italian lessons. That is impossible!'

Nick Kendall looked pleased.

'I am glad you want to help Mrs Ashley,' he said. 'The bank

32

can pay some money to her every quarter[45]. How much do you suggest?'

When I told him, my godfather looked surprised. 'That may be too much, Philip,' he said slowly.

'Ambrose would have wanted me to be generous[46],' I said. 'Write me a letter for her, and write a letter to the bank.'

'You are as impulsive[47] as Ambrose,' Nick Kendall said. But he wrote the letters.

'I will take the letter to the bank,' I said. 'But I don't want cousin Rachel to know that I have arranged this. Will you send a servant to my house with the letter for her?'

Nick Kendall agreed.

As I was leaving, I saw Louise. 'I can't stop,' I said at once. 'I have come on business.'

Louise looked at me coldly.

'And how is Mrs Ashley?' she asked.

'Well and happy,' I answered. 'She is very busy in the garden today.'

'I am surprised that you are not helping her,' Louise said. 'I'm sure Mrs Ashley can make you do exactly what she wants.'

Louise made me feel very angry and I left the house without another word.

———

I rode to the bank and gave them the letter. I didn't get home until nearly four o'clock. I did not see my cousin Rachel. I rang the bell for Seecombe. He told me that Mrs Ashley had worked in the gardens until three o'clock. Then she had asked for water for a bath.

I decided to take a bath too and I asked for an early dinner. Later, I went to my cousin Rachel's sitting-room. I was feeling very happy.

She was sitting on a stool by the fire. She had washed her hair and she was drying it.

'Come and sit down,' she said. 'Why are you staring at me? Have you never seen a woman brushing her hair before? Wait here, while I go and change my dress for dinner.'

My cousin Rachel was in her bedroom when Seecombe came in with the letter from my godfather. I stood up, feeling awkward. There was no sound from the bedroom as my cousin Rachel read the letter. Then suddenly, she came out of the room. She looked very angry.

'You made Mr Kendall write this letter,' she said. 'Did you think I was asking you for money? I am angry and ashamed[48].'

'Ashamed?' I repeated. 'I would be ashamed if Mrs Ambrose Ashley had to give Italian lessons. What would people think of Ambrose? The money is yours, take it.'

I was angry now. We stood staring at each other. Then my cousin Rachel's eyes filled with tears. She turned, went quickly into her bedroom and shut the door loudly.

———

That night, I had dinner alone. Is that how women behaved? Did they always cry when they were angry? Thank God I had no wife! Poor Ambrose! No wonder he had been unhappy. I knew I would never marry now.

After dinner, I read, and then fell asleep in my chair. When I woke up, it was time to go upstairs to my room.

On the table by my bed was a note from my cousin Rachel.
Dear Philip,

Please forgive me for my rudeness. I have written to Mr Kendall thanking him for his letter. I thank you too.

Rachel.

The door to her sitting-room was open. I walked straight through and knocked on the bedroom door. The room was in darkness, but I could see my cousin Rachel in bed.

'I want to thank you for your note and say goodnight,' I said. 'I'm sorry I made you angry. I did not want you to cry.'

'I cried because of what you said about Ambrose,' she said. 'I will take the money, Philip, but after this week, I must go.

'But I thought you liked it here,' I said. 'You seemed so happy, working in the garden . . . You have a home here. If Ambrose had made another will, this would have been your home.'

'Oh God!' she cried. 'Why do you think I came?'

I looked down at her. She looked very young, very alone.

'I don't know why you came,' I said. 'But I know Ambrose would have wished you to stay, perhaps to plan the gardens . . .'

'Very well. I'll stay – for a time,' she said.

'Then you aren't angry with me any more?'

'I was never angry with you, Philip, but you are sometimes very stupid. Come closer.'

As I bent down, she took my face between her hands and kissed me.

'Now go to bed, like a good boy, and sleep well,' she said.

I moved to the door like a man in a dream. When I was back in my room, I wrote a short note to Nick Kendall. I told him that my cousin Rachel would take the money. Then I walked down to the hall to put my letter in the post bag. In the morning, Seecombe would arrange for the letters to be delivered.

There were two letters in the bag. Both had been written by my cousin Rachel. One was addressed to my godfather, Nick Kendall. The other was addressed to Signor Rainaldi, in Florence. I stared at it, before putting it back in the bag.

Why had my cousin Rachel written to Signor Rainaldi? What did she have to tell him?

9

We Open Ambrose's Boxes

Now it was October, but the weather was fine and my cousin Rachel was able to work in the garden. We also had time to visit the tenants[49] on the estate. They all loved my cousin Rachel. When they were ill, she gave them medicines made from herbs[50].

Sometimes in the afternoons, our neighbours came to the house. Sometimes my cousin Rachel went to visit them. I enjoyed listening to her at dinner. My cousin Rachel told me about the people she had seen during the day. She always made me laugh.

But at the end of the month, the weather changed. Rain fell every day. There was no gardening and no visiting.

One morning, my cousin Rachel and I were standing at the library window. Outside the rain was falling heavily. Then Seecombe reminded us about Ambrose's boxes. They were still in my room and had never been emptied. We began to open the boxes. The first box we opened was full of Ambrose's clothes. Suddenly my cousin Rachel was crying. Then she was in my arms, her head against my chest.

'Oh Philip! I'm so sorry,' she said. 'But we both loved him so much.'

I moved my lips against her hair.

'Don't worry, Rachel,' I said. 'I'll do this.'

It was the first time I had called her by her name. She stopped crying and we continued to unpack the boxes. We decided to give Ambrose's clothes to the tenants on the estate. Then we began to look at the books.

As I opened a book on gardening, a piece of paper fell out. It looked like part of a letter, written by Ambrose.

She cannot stop spending money, I read. It is like an illness. If this goes on, my dear Philip, she will spend everything. You must tell Kendall in case . . .

'What have you there?' my cousin Rachel said suddenly. 'That is Ambrose's writing.'

'It's nothing,' I said and threw the piece of paper on the fire. We continued our work in silence.

That same morning, some boxes had arrived for my cousin Rachel from London. New dresses, perhaps. I remembered the words in Ambrose's letter: *It is like an illness. She will spend everything.*

After dinner, when we went to the library as usual, the most beautiful blue and gold cloth lay over the chairs.

'Do you like it, Philip?' my cousin Rachel asked. 'It's Italian. It will make beautiful curtains for your room.'

'Isn't it very expensive?' I asked.

'Well, yes, but that isn't important. If you like it, take it – as a present from me.'

I thought unhappily about the letter, but I could say nothing.

As we sat by the fire, my cousin Rachel began talking about her life in Italy. She spoke of the time before she had met Ambrose. I was listening with the greatest interest, when she suddenly said, 'What was on that paper you threw in the fire, Philip?'

'It was from a letter,' I said, 'Ambrose was worried about money – I can't remember exactly.' The worried look went from Rachel's eyes.

'Was that all?' she said. 'Poor Ambrose. He did not understand life in Italy. He thought I spent too much money. He was very generous until he became ill. Then he changed so much.'

'How did he change?' I asked.

'When I wanted money for the house, he became very angry. In the end I had to ask Rainaldi for money to pay the servants. When Ambrose found out, he refused to have Rainaldi in the house.

'It was a terrible time. I did not want to tell you about it, Philip. Ambrose was so ill. He trusted no one. You wouldn't have known him.'

'That is all over now,' I said. 'Don't make yourself unhappy. You cannot bring Ambrose back. This is your home now.'

My cousin Rachel looked into my eyes. 'You are so like him,' she said. 'Sometimes I am afraid. You must not change too.'

I took her hands in mine.

'I will never change,' I said. 'And we must remember Ambrose as he used to be. 'This house belongs to all three of us now.'

'You are very good to me, Philip,' my cousin Rachel said as she moved to the door. 'I hope that one day you will be as happy as I was with Ambrose – at the beginning.'

She went to bed and I sat alone by the library fire. My terrible jealousy had returned. But now I was jealous of Ambrose. I was jealous because of the love that my cousin Rachel had given him.

10

A *Christmas Present*

In the past, I had always disliked the winter. But with my cousin Rachel in the house, things were very different. When I was with my cousin Rachel, I was happy. When she was away from the house, I was bored. Life was dull and uninteresting until she returned.

Like everyone else, I now thought that my cousin Rachel was beautiful. Whenever she came into a room, she made it a happier, more interesting place.

In the evenings, we sat together in her small sitting-room. We drank tisana as she and Ambrose had done in Florence. The evenings were the best times. But when I went to my room, I could not sleep. Any day, perhaps, my cousin Rachel would decide to go to London. If she left me, I would feel terribly alone.

When Ambrose had been at home, he had always given dinner to the tenants on Christmas Eve. This year, I decided to do the same.

My cousin Rachel was very pleased. At once, she began to make preparations. Packages arrived from London – presents perhaps – she began to plan the Christmas meal.

One thing worried me. What could I give my cousin Rachel for a present? I thought about it for a long time and at last I had an idea. I remembered the jewels that belonged to my family. They were kept in the bank for safety. In three months' time, on my birthday, they would be mine. But I did not want to wait that long. And I remembered that Nick Kendall had gone to London.

I went to the bank that day and asked the manager to show me the Ashley jewels.

They were very beautiful – blue, green and red. But my cousin Rachel always wore black. She could not wear coloured jewels with mourning clothes[51].

Then I saw the collar of pearls[52]. How beautiful the white pearls would look on my cousin Rachel's neck!

'Your mother was the last woman to wear this collar,' the manager said. 'All the brides[53] of the Ashley family wear it on their wedding-day.'

I put out my hand and took the collar. 'I will take this with me,' I said.

The manager looked worried. 'The pearls are not yours until the 1st of April,' he said. 'I don't think Mr Kendall would like you to take them away.'

'I'll speak to Mr Kendall,' I said. I put the collar in its box and stood up. I knew the pearls were the right present for my cousin Rachel. I felt very excited.

Then at last, it was Christmas Eve. Seecombe had brought a tree into the house and had decorated[54] it as usual. Dinner was to start at five. After dinner, everybody would have a present. This year, my cousin Rachel was going to give out the presents with me.

Before I dressed for dinner, I sent the collar of pearls to her room. With it, was a note: *My mother was the last woman to wear this. Now it belongs to you. I want you to wear it tonight and always. Philip.*

When I was ready, I went downstairs and waited for my cousin Rachel. She came in slowly. Her dress was black, but it was one I had not seen before. The collar of pearls was round her neck. I had never seen her look so happy or so beautiful.

She put her arms around me and then she kissed me. She

kissed me not as a cousin, but as a lover. This is what Ambrose died for, I thought. And for this I would happily die too.

She gave me her hand and we walked in to dinner.

At first, I thought this was going to be the happiest evening of my life. I remember the food, the noise and the excitement. My cousin Rachel had bought everyone a small present, carefully chosen. Mine was a gold chain for my keys with our initials, P.A.R.A. hanging from it.

Our plates and glasses were filled, emptied and filled again. Then we gave everyone a present from the tree.

When dinner was over, I spoke to my godfather, Nick Kendall, for the first time that evening.

'Good evening, sir, and happy Christmas,' I said. Nick

Kendall looked angry and he said nothing. He was staring at the collar of pearls around my cousin's neck.

Then at last, the tenants had all left. Louise and my cousin Rachel went upstairs. And I found myself alone with my godfather.

'I have some bad news from the bank,' he said. 'The manager tells me that Mrs Ashley is already several hundred pounds overdrawn[55]. I don't understand it. She must be sending money back to Italy.'

'She is very generous,' I said. 'And there were debts in Florence, I think. You must give Mrs Ashley more money.'

Nick Kendall looked unhappy. 'There is something else, Philip,' he said. 'You should not have taken that collar of pearls. It is not yours.'

'It will be mine in three months' time,' I said quickly. 'My cousin Rachel will take good care of it.'

'I am not so sure,' Nick Kendall said. 'I have been hearing stories about Mrs Ashley and her first husband. They were both well-known for their bad lives. They spent money carelessly.'

'That can't be true!' I cried.

'True or not,' my godfather replied. 'I'm afraid that collar must go back to the bank.'

'But I gave it to my cousin Rachel as a present. She has a right to wear the collar.'

'Only if Ambrose had lived,' Nick Kendall said. 'That collar of pearls is worn by the Ashley brides, no one else. If you do not ask Mrs Ashley to give it back, I will.'

Then suddenly, my cousin Rachel and Louise were in the room.

'You are quite right, Mr Kendall,' my cousin Rachel said. 'I was very proud to wear the collar and now I shall give it back.' And she took off the collar and gave it to my godfather.

'Thank you, Mrs Ashley,' he said. 'And now Louise and I must go. We wish you both a happy Christmas.'

When they had gone, my cousin Rachel held out her arms. I went up to her.

'I'm so sorry,' I said. 'Everything has gone wrong. My mother wore those pearls on her wedding-day, that is why I wanted you to have them. Don't you understand?'

'Of course I do, Philip dear,' she said. 'If Ambrose and I had been married here, he would have given them to me on my wedding-day.'

I said nothing. My cousin Rachel had not understood. I was thinking of another wedding-day, a wedding-day in the future . . .

11

Rainaldi Again

The New Year began and my birthday – on 1st April – was three months away. How I wanted to have control of my own money! I was tired of Nick Kendall being my guardian.

However, I could spend money on the house. I decided to make it beautiful for Rachel. There were many repairs to be done. From January, I had nearly twenty men working for me. The bills for the work were sent to my godfather.

Rachel and I had many plans for the gardens too. Work had started on a sunken water-garden[56]. We had found the design for the water-garden in one of Rachel's books.

Because there were so many workmen in the house, we could not have visitors. My cousin Rachel and I stayed quietly at home and I was very happy. I loved to watch Rachel move about the house. I loved to hear her voice. When her hands touched me, my heart beat faster.

The first days of spring came and the sun shone. Then

something happened which took all my happiness away again.

I had kept one of Ambrose's old coats to wear myself. One day, as I was walking in the woods, I felt something in a pocket. It was another letter from Ambrose.

I was pleased that I was alone. I walked on until I reached the highest place on the estate. Ambrose had always loved to sit there. I sat down and held the letter in my hands. I did not want to open it. I was afraid that Ambrose had written something bad about Rachel. We were so happy together now that I wanted to forget the past. But at last, I opened the letter. It had been written three months before his death, but he had never posted it.

My cousin Rachel, Ambrose wrote, had been expecting a child, but it had died. The doctors told her that she could never have another child. At first, Rachel was quiet and unhappy. Then she began to spend money carelessly. Ambrose suspected that Rainaldi was in love with her. For these reasons, Ambrose had not signed his new will, in which he left everything to Rachel.

Ambrose also wrote about his terrible headaches. He told me about the fever which at first made him violent[57]. Then it made him very weak. Ambrose was very unhappy and he had written: *You are the only person who can help me, Philip. Are Rachel and Rainaldi trying to poison me for my money? I must know!*

I hid the terrible letter under a large stone and walked slowly back to the house. I could not forget Ambrose's words. But I decided that Rachel must never know about the letter.

In three weeks' time the estate and all the money would be mine. But this was not right. Ambrose had made a new will, but he had not signed it because of his illness. His money belonged to Rachel. She must have it.

That night, I asked Rachel about Ambrose's will. She showed me a copy of it, which I read carefully. Everything had been left to Rachel. Then if she had died without children, everything was to be mine.

'Why did Ambrose not sign this will?' I asked. 'Tell me, Rachel.'

'I don't know,' she answered quietly. 'Perhaps when he knew we could not have children, his feelings changed. Perhaps it was only a mistake. But when the headaches started, Ambrose suspected me of terrible things. I can't speak about that time. Please leave me alone, Philip. I can't answer any more questions.'

'I have reasons for my questions,' I said. 'You will understand in three weeks' time.'

By the following morning, I had made up my mind. I rode into the town and, with the help of a lawyer, wrote out a document. In three weeks' time, all my property would be given to Mrs Rachel Ashley. The jewels would belong to her too. But she would not be able to sell the house or the land.

'I have one question,' the lawyer said. 'Mrs Ashley is quite a young woman. What will happen to the property if she marries again?'

I thought for a moment. The house and the estate must always belong to the Ashleys. 'If she marries,' I said, 'or if she dies, the property becomes mine again. That must be made clear.'

I told the lawyer that the document must be kept secret. He promised to send me a copy on the last day of March.

I felt very happy as I rode home. My dear Rachel would never leave me now. We would live in perfect happiness forever.

When I reached the house, I heard voices in the library. The door opened and Rachel came out, laughing happily.

'Come and see my visitor, Philip,' she cried. 'He has come a long way to see us both.'

The man stood up and held out his hand.

It was Rainaldi. We stood there, looking at each other. Then Rainaldi began talking about his journey. Rachel suggested that he should stay in the house for a few days. I could say nothing.

During dinner, Rachel and Rainaldi talked about people and places I knew nothing about. Often, they spoke in Italian and I could not understand a word.

At last, Rachel stood up and said, 'You must excuse us, Philip. Rainaldi and I have some business to discuss. He has brought papers I must sign.'

They went upstairs and I walked alone in the gardens. I felt cold and unhappy. I stayed outside until the light went out in Rainaldi's room. I had just reached my own room when there was a quiet knock on my door.

'I came to wish you goodnight,' my cousin Rachel said. 'Why didn't you come and drink tisana with us, Philip? You must make Rainaldi welcome. He is a very old friend of mine.'

Rainaldi stayed with us for seven days. As he laughed and talked with Rachel, I began to hate him. When it was time for Rainaldi to leave, he took my cousin Rachel's hand and kissed it.

'Write and tell me your plans,' he said. 'I shall be in London for some time.'

'I am making no plans until after the first of April,' Rachel replied with a laugh.

Rainaldi smiled. 'I hope Philip enjoys his birthday,' he said. '1st April is All Fools' Day[58], isn't it? But perhaps Philip doesn't want to remember that.'

When Rainaldi had gone, Rachel smiled at me. 'You have been very good, Philip,' she said. 'Are you glad we are alone again?'

12

All Fools' Day

As my birthday came nearer, I became more and more excited. Rachel laughed at me. 'You are like a child!' she said. 'What plans are you making for the day?'

But I had made no plans. All I wanted was that Rachel should know about the document. And one more thing – Rachel should have all the family jewels. I went to the bank myself. I brought them back to the house and hid them in my room.

On the last day of March, I rode over to Nick Kendall. First, I handed him a copy of Ambrose's will. My godfather looked at it carefully.

'I don't understand why Ambrose didn't sign it,' he said. 'But we have done all we can for Mrs Ashley.'

'I don't agree,' I said. 'I want to make everything right.' And I handed him a copy of the document the lawyer had prepared.

'Read this,' I said. 'And remember that my cousin Rachel knows nothing about it.'

'I wish Signor Rainaldi had seen this,' Nick Kendall said slowly. 'He told me how careless Mrs Ashley is with money. This document of yours gives her great power over the property. I have to ask you one question, Philip. Are you in love with Mrs Ashley?'

My face went red.

'I am only doing what Ambrose wanted,' I said.

'Perhaps,' Nick Kendall answered. 'But people are talking. Mrs Ashley should leave, get married again. She might marry you if you asked her.'

'I am sure she would not,' I said.

Nick Kendall watched me sadly as I signed my name on the document.

'There are some women who bring sadness to all those who love them,' he said. 'They cannot help it. I think Mrs Ashley is one of those women.'

The sun was setting as I rode home. I bathed, changed my clothes and went into the dining-room. Rachel wanted to know where I had been. But I laughed and told her nothing.

After dinner, I was too excited to sit still. I walked down to the sea. There was a moon and the night was warm. I took off my clothes and for a few minutes I swam in the ice-cold water.

When I got back to the house, it was five minutes to twelve. I could not wait any longer. I stood under Rachel's window and called her name. When she looked out, I said, 'I have something for you, Rachel.'

Then I ran to my room for the jewels.

'I want you to have these now,' I said. 'Listen, the clock is striking twelve and it is the first of April. I am twenty-five and I can do what I like.'

I put the document on her table and began to open the boxes of jewels. Rachel's eyes opened wide in surprise and suddenly we

I put the document on her table and began to open the boxes of jewels.

were laughing together. I put the pearl collar round her neck. As I looked at her, I remembered the other Ashley women who had worn it.

'You have given me so much,' Rachel said at last. 'I have only a small present for you. What else can I give you? Tell me.'

'There is one thing,' I said. I looked into her dark eyes. They shone very brightly in the candle-light. She laughed softly and blew out the candle. We were alone in the darkness.

I did not leave her room until sunrise. Happiness had come to me at last. Rachel accepted me and my love. She was the first woman I ever loved – and she was the last.

I remember walking alone in the garden as the birds began to sing. Rachel and I would be always together now – day after day, night after night, for all our lives.

I went back to my room and slept. After breakfast, I went into the garden again. I picked the most beautiful flowers I could find.

Rachel was in bed, eating her breakfast. I threw the flowers on the bed in front of her.

'Good morning, again,' I said. 'I have come to say one thing– I love you.'

Rachel looked up at me without smiling. 'You should not come into my room so early,' she said. 'The servants will talk.'

I smiled, but said nothing. I went downstairs. I wanted to tell the servants that Rachel and I were going to be married. Then I decided that we would tell them together, later.

I walked in the gardens until it was time for Rachel to leave her room. The day was fine and I decided we should go out riding. But when I got back to the house, Rachel had already left. I waited for a long time, but she did not return. At last, I walked along the road, hoping to meet her.

When I saw the carriage, I stopped it. I got in and sat down beside Rachel. She was wearing a veil[59] and I could not see her face.

'Where have you been?' I asked her.

'To see your godfather.'

'You cannot change anything,' I told her. 'I am twenty-five. Everything I have is yours.'

'Yes, I understand that now,' Rachel said. 'But I wanted to be sure.'

Her voice was quiet. I did not think she was smiling.

'Let me look at your face,' I said.

She lifted her veil. There was no love in her eyes now.

'I think Louise was a little more friendly today,' Rachel said. 'She will make you a good wife. We made plans to meet in London together.'

I looked at her in surprise. It was unkind of her to make jokes about Louise. And why was Rachel talking about London? We had made no plans to go there.

'Come into the woods, Rachel,' I whispered. 'I want to kiss you so much.'

She did not answer, but took something out of her bag. 'Here is your present,' she said, and she gave me a small, gold pin for my tie. 'If I had known about the money, I would have bought something larger.'

As I dressed for dinner, I could think of only one thing. Money is the one way to please her . . . the one way to please her . . .

When we sat down together for my birthday dinner, Rachel was wearing the pearl collar. We both drank wine and I started to feel happier. Time would soon pass. When the mourning time was over, Rachel would be my wife . . .

While we were sitting at the table, the Kendalls came into the room. When they had wished me a happy birthday, I stood up, my glass in my hand.

'From this morning, I have been the happiest of men,' I said. 'I want you to be the first to know. Rachel has promised to be my wife.'

I smiled at them all. But Rachel's face was hard and cold.

'Have you gone mad, Philip?' she said. She looked at the Kendalls. 'You must forgive[60] him, he has drunk too much wine. I'm sure he will apologize[61].'

Rachel got up and the others followed her out of the room. I stood without moving until I heard them leave the house. When Rachel came back, we stared at each other without speaking.

Then Rachel said, 'You had better go to bed, Philip, before you say any more foolish things.'

'Foolish?' I repeated. 'But last night . . . Surely you love me, Rachel? Last night you proved that you loved me. It was a promise of marriage . . .'

'No, Philip, I had no thought of marriage. I was thanking you for the jewels, that was all. There was no love.'

I looked at her hard, cold face. I began to understand what Ambrose had suffered. She had everything. What else could I do? Suddenly I wanted to frighten her, to show her my strength. I put my hands round her neck and looked into her eyes.

'Will you marry me now?' I whispered.

Her dark eyes were full of fear, but she did not speak. I loosened my fingers. There were red marks on her white skin.

Rachel turned and went upstairs. I followed her, but she was too quick for me. She closed her door and locked it.

As she stood there, I saw myself in a mirror on the wall. There I stood, tall, awkward, white faced. But was it myself or Ambrose standing there?

As I lay in bed, I heard the clock strike midnight. All Fools' Day was over.

13

Louise . . . and Laburnum Trees

When I went down to breakfast in the morning, there was a note for me on the table. It was not from Rachel, but from Louise.

Dear Philip,

I was sorry for you last night. If you want a friend to talk to, please let me know.

Louise.

At first, I did not want to see Louise. But I had not slept all night and I was very unhappy. Louise knew me well. I sent her a note asking her to meet me in the church that morning.

'I have been worried about you for a long time,' Louise told me. 'She has deceived[62] you from the beginning.'

'I made a mistake,' I said.

'But Mrs Ashley did not,' Louise replied. 'She came here to get the money. She stayed until she got it. That is all.'

'I don't believe you!' I cried. 'She came on impulse. She stayed because she was happy here.'

'No, she had a plan,' Louise replied. 'She has been sending money back to Italy all the winter. She waited until you were twenty-five. But then you made her a present of everything. You made things easy for her.'

'I know you don't like Rachel,' I said. 'That is why you are saying these things. But I have asked her to marry me. And I shall go on asking her.'

'But she will never marry you,' Louise said with a sad smile. 'When you gave Mrs Ashley the document, she went straight to my father. She asked him if everything now belonged to her. My father told her that that was true. But he warned her that if she married again, she would lose the money. She told him she had no plans to marry again.'

'But if she marries me, she will lose nothing,' I said.

'She would not be able to go back to Italy, or send money there,' Louise said quietly.

She looked at me and said, 'I will go now, Philip. I have upset you deeply. I am very sorry.'

As I rode home, the rain began to fall heavily. When I got back, I was cold and wet. There was a note from Rachel in my room.

I have asked Mary Pascoe to stay here with me. After last night, I cannot be alone with you again.

Mary Pascoe, the vicar's daughter? Mary Pascoe was a large, plain girl. Rachel and I had often laughed about her. I could not believe it.

But it was true. This was the punishment for my one moment of anger. Whenever I was with Rachel, Mary Pascoe was there too. Oh, God, what had I done?

By dinner-time, I was feeling very ill. I went upstairs to my room. I got into bed and the sheets felt very cold. I hoped that Rachel would come to me, but she did not.

In the morning, I tried to dress, but I was too weak. My neck was stiff and there was a terrible pain in my head. When I called for

Seecombe he took one look at me and hurried out of the room. Then my cousin Rachel was there, her face very white.

'I will not hurt you, Rachel,' I said. 'Please send Mary Pascoe home.'

'Don't talk now, lie still,' Rachel answered.

Then the room was dark. The doctor came. I was hot, then cold. I called for Rachel and she held my hand. 'I am with you,' she said. I closed my eyes.

———

When I awoke, the room was full of light and warmth. How long had I been asleep? Rachel was sitting near my bed. I put my hand to my face.

'I have grown a beard!' I said. I began to laugh. At once, Rachel was holding a glass to my lips. She made me drink the bitter liquid.

'Have you sent Mary Pascoe away?' I asked. Rachel looked surprised.

'She went away five weeks ago,' she answered. 'You have been so ill that you nearly died. The doctors could not help you. Your strength and my medicines saved you.'

I lay there, with her hand in mine. I could not speak. Five weeks had passed and I could remember nothing! Only that Rachel and I had been married on the day before my birthday. We had kept our marriage a secret. But in two months' time, Rachel would be out of mourning and we would be able to tell everyone.

I was very weak for a long time. But the weather was good and I was soon able to go into the garden.

The workmen had been busy for many months. They had dug out the ground to make the sunken water-garden. It was very deep, but it was not yet finished. Yellow flowers hung on the laburnum trees that Rachel had planted. I remembered the laburnum tree at the Villa Sangalletti and the green, poisonous seeds lying under it.

That evening, as Rachel and I were drinking our tisana, I said, 'I heard something strange today. Seecombe told me you were going back to Florence. I thought you had sold the villa.'

'No, I have enough money to keep it now. I shall probably stay there for the winter. Perhaps you could visit me in the spring.'

'Visit you?' I repeated. 'But a husband should be with his wife always.'

Rachel sat very still.

'Your wife? Oh, God, Philip,' she whispered. 'What do you mean? We are not married.'

'But we are,' I said. 'I remember clearly . . .' But as I spoke, the pain returned to my head. I suddenly knew that our marriage was a dream.

'Why didn't you let me die?' I cried. 'I cannot live here alone, I cannot.'

I looked at her face.

'Give me a few weeks, only a few weeks,' I said.

She did not reply.

14

What is the Truth?

The summer came, but Rachel did not speak of leaving. I became stronger. But sometimes the terrible pain in my head came back and I could not think clearly. But I told Rachel nothing about it.

Then Rachel began to drive into the town – two or three times a week. When I asked her about these visits, she told me that she had a lot of business to do.

One day when Rachel was busy at home, I rode into the town alone. It was Saturday and the streets were full of people. As I walked slowly through the town, a man came out of an inn[63]. He stood in the doorway for a moment, looking up and down the street. It was Rainaldi.

That evening, as Rachel was going up to her room after dinner, I stopped her.

'How long has Rainaldi been in the town?' I asked. 'Why is he here?'

'Because he is my friend,' Rachel answered. 'I know you hate him and do not want him here. Ambrose was jealous of him. Are you too?'

'Yes,' I said. 'I hate Rainaldi, because he is in love with you. Send him away.'

'Certainly not,' she said. 'I need him. I will have him here if I wish – the house is mine.'

In my anger, I took a step towards her.

'Don't touch me!' she cried. 'That is how Ambrose behaved. I can't suffer it again . . .'

I turned away. 'If you want to see Rainaldi, ask him here,' I said. 'Don't go secretly into the town to meet him.'

And so Rainaldi came to stay in the house. He behaved politely but I could not bear to see them together. They always spoke in Italian and she looked at him all the time.

Food seemed to have no taste now. The tisana I drank with them in the evenings tasted bitter. Then the fever returned again. I was sick and too weak to stand. I had to stay in bed for a few days. When I was better again, Rachel told me that Rainaldi had gone back to Italy.

'When are you going there?' I asked.

Rachel did not reply.

A day or two later, a letter arrived for Rachel in Rainaldi's handwriting. As I drank tisana with Rachel that evening, I saw the letter on her desk. Was it a love-letter? I had to know.

That night, when Rachel was in bed, I crept into her sitting-room and searched the desk. The letter was not there. But in one small drawer, I found an envelope. Inside it were some small, green seeds. They were laburnum seeds, poisonous to animals and to men.

I put back the envelope and returned to my room. There were two bottles of medicine on the table. I poured the medicines out of the window. Then I went downstairs. The cups from which we had drunk our tisana had not been washed. Did the liquid in my cup have a bitter taste? I could not be sure.

I went to bed and lay there thinking. I was not angry, but I was very unhappy. I remembered Ambrose's words: *Are they trying to poison me? . . . Rachel has won – I am dying . . .*

The following day was Sunday. Rachel and I went to church as usual. As she sat beside me, her face was calm and happy. I wished I could hate her, but I could not.

After church, Rachel went to speak to Mary Pascoe. A workman came up to me and said, 'Excuse me, Mr Ashley, but I wanted to warn you. Don't walk on the new bridge over the sunken garden. It is not finished yet. Anyone walking on it would fall and break their neck!'

'Thank you,' I said. 'I will remember.'

At dinner, Rachel was kinder than she had been for a long time. She talked about Florence. She said she would look for a stone statue there to make a fountain for the sunken garden. She made tisana as usual, but I refused to drink it. I would never again drink anything she gave me.

'But it is good for you, Philip,' she said.

'No,' I said. 'You drink it.'

'I have drunk mine already,' Rachel said. 'I will pour this away.'

We talked together for half an hour or so and then Rachel said, 'I think I shall walk for a little. I want to look at the sunken garden. Will you come with me, Philip?'

I shook my head. 'Take care, Rachel,' I said.

'Of what?' she answered with a smile. 'There is no danger here, Philip.'

I sat by the window until it was almost dark. Rachel had not returned. At last, I ran out of the house and down to the sunken garden. The bridge was broken. My cousin Rachel lay on the ground below. I climbed down and held her hands in mine. They were cold.

My cousin Rachel lay on the ground below.

'Rachel,' I said. She opened her eyes and I thought she knew me. But she called me Ambrose. I held her hands until she died.

———

You know now who killed Rachel. But how did Ambrose die? Did Rachel kill him? I shall go on asking myself that question until the day I die.

I live alone now. I am a young man, but I think only of the past. The two people I loved are dead. I have an empty life in front of me. That is my punishment and it is worse than death.

POINTS
FOR
UNDERSTANDING

Points for Understanding

1

1 The writer of the story is called Philip Ashley. How did Ambrose Ashley become Philip's guardian?
2 What kind of house did Ambrose live in?
3 Who was Ambrose Ashley's heir?
4 Why has Philip Ashley written this story?
5 What does Philip Ashley ask the reader of this story to decide?

2

1 The weather was bad for Ambrose.
   (a) What did the doctors tell Ambrose he must do?
   (b) What did the doctors say would happen if Ambrose took their advice?
2 At Christmas, Ambrose wrote a letter from Florence.
   (a) Why did Ambrose call the woman he had met in Florence 'cousin Rachel'?
   (b) What had happened to cousin Rachel's husband?
   (c) What was the name of cousin Rachel's house?
   (d) Why was Philip pleased that Ambrose had found a friend?
3 . . . the next letter did not arrive until the early spring.
   (a) What was Ambrose giving cousin Rachel advice about?
   (b) Why did this letter surprise Philip?
4 Then, at the end of April, I received the letter that changed my whole life.
   (a) What did Philip learn from this letter?
   (b) How did Philip feel when he read this letter?
   (c) What did the neighbours say when they heard the news?
5 Nick Kendall – a lawyer – was Philip's godfather. Louise was Nick Kendall's daughter.
   (a) How long had Philip and Louise known each other?
   (b) What advice did Nick Kendall give Philip when he was told the news about Ambrose and cousin Rachel?
   (c) What was Philip thinking while Nick Kendall was giving him this advice?

6 Ambrose was having terrible headaches in Italy that summer. Why was that unusual?
7 Nick Kendall told Philip: 'These are the words of a very sick man.'
   (a)   What words of Ambrose was Nick Kendall talking about?
   (b)   What reason did Nick Kendall give for the way Ambrose had written?
   (c)   What did they decide Philip must do?
8 . . . a last letter arrived from Ambrose.
   (a)   What did Ambrose ask Philip to do?
   (b)   What did Ambrose call cousin Rachel in this letter?

3

1 What did Philip Ashley learn when he arrived at the Villa Sangalletti?
2 What kind of tree was growing beside the pool in the courtyard of the villa?
3. The servant told Philip: 'In the summer, they always sat here, Signor Ashley and the contessa.'
   (a)   Where did Ambrose and cousin Rachel sit?
   (b)   What did they drink after dinner every day?
4 When he was ill, Ambrose had acted very strangely. What had he done?
5 Philip asked the servant: 'What happened to his clothes?'
   (a)   What did the servant reply?
   (b)   Where was cousin Rachel?
   (c)   Where was Ambrose buried?
   (d)   What did the servant's wife give Philip?

4

1 Philip showed Rainaldi the last two letters from Ambrose.
   (a)   What explanation did Rainaldi give for the way Ambrose had written?
   (b)   Who had given the same explanation?
2 How did Rainaldi know that Nick Kendall was now Philip's guardian?
3 Philip said to Rainaldi: 'If I had been here, Ambrose would be alive now.' What did Rainaldi reply?
4 Philip did not believe Rainaldi's story.
   (a)   What did Philip believe about Ambrose's death?
   (b)   What did Philip promise to do one day?

5

1 When Philip was back in England, Nick Kendall came to the Ashley house to explain Ambrose's will.
   (a) At what age would Philip Ashley own the Ashley house and estate?
   (b) How many months would Philip have to wait?
   (c) What would Philip have to do if he needed money?
   (d) What did Nick Kendall hope Philip would do one day?
2 What would have happened if Ambrose had changed his will when he married?
3 Nick Kendall said to Philip: 'Keep these ideas to yourself.' What ideas was Nick Kendall talking about?
4 Louise said to Philip: 'No woman has stayed in that house for twenty years.'
   (a) What did Louise think was wrong with the Ashley house?
   (b) What did Philip reply?
   (c) What did Philip decide to do when he got home?
   (d) Who was moving into Ambrose's room?
5 There was a portrait of Ambrose on one wall.
   (a) When had the portrait been painted?
   (b) Who had Ambrose looked like?
6 Why did Philip go out walking until after six o'clock?
7 'Where is her luggage?' Philip asked Seecombe.
   (a) Where was cousin Rachel's luggage?
   (b) What other boxes had arrived with cousin Rachel?
   (c) Where had these boxes been put?

6

1 Cousin Rachel said to Philip: 'I was longing to be h . . . here.' What did cousin Rachel nearly say instead of 'here'?
2 Cousin Rachel said: 'You're nearly asleep, Philip. Hadn't you better go to bed?' What did Philip ask himself?
3 Already Philip's ideas about cousin Rachel were changing.
   (a) Why did cousin Rachel ask Philip to go quickly?
   (b) How were Philip's ideas about cousin Rachel changing?

7

1 Philip found Tamlyn, the head gardener, and cousin Rachel putting new plants into the ground. What plants were they?
2 Cousin Rachel said to Philip: 'I would like you to see the garden at Villa Sangalletti.' Why was Philip surprised?
3 At that moment, I felt that my cousin Rachel knew everything.
    (a)   What had cousin Rachel finished reading?
    (b)   What did Philip mean by 'knew everything'?
    (c)   How did Philip feel about cousin Rachel now that he had met her?
    (d)   What reason did Philip give for his earlier feelings to cousin Rachel?
4 Cousin Rachel told Philip: 'You were right to hate me.'
    (a)   What did cousin Rachel mean when she said that Philip was right to hate her?
    (b)   Why had cousin Rachel grown tired of hearing Philip's name?
5 What did Rachel do as she and Philip stood on the stairs?

8

1 Cousin Rachel told Philip: 'A man needs a wife when he is entertaining.'
    (a)   Who did cousin Rachel think Philip was going to marry?
    (b)   What did Philip say to this idea?
    (c)   What did Philip want Rachel to do?
2 Cousin Rachel said to Philip: 'It would be better if I gave your neighbours Italian lessons.'
    (a)   Why would cousin Rachel have to give Italian lessons?
    (b)   What did Philip say in reply?
    (c)   Why did Philip stay away from the house until it was dark?
    (d)   What idea did Philip have while he was walking?
3 Why did Philip not want cousin Rachel to know that he was going to Nick Kendall's house?
4 Nick Kendall told Philip: 'You are as impulsive as Ambrose.' What did he mean?
5 Cousin Rachel said to Philip: 'You made Mr Kendall write this letter.'
    (a)   What did the letter say?
    (b)   How did cousin Rachel say she felt about the letter?
    (c)   What did Philip say to her in reply?
    (d)   What did cousin Rachel write later in a note to Philip?

6 Cousin Rachel told Philip she was going to leave the Ashley house at the end of that week. What did Philip reply?
7 In the post-bag, Philip noticed two other letters in cousin Rachel's handwriting.
   (a)   Why had Rachel written a letter to Nick Kendall?
   (b)   Who was the other letter addressed to?
   (c)   Why did the name on the other letter puzzle Philip?

9

1 What kind of medicines did cousin Rachel give the tenants when they were ill?
2 Philip remembered the words in Ambrose's letter.
   (a)   Where had Philip found Ambrose's letter?
   (b)   What arrived in the house that morning?
   (c)   What had Ambrose written in the letter?
   (d)   What did Philip do with the letter?
3 Cousin Rachel told Philip: 'Then Ambrose changed so much.'
   (a)   How had Ambrose changed?
   (b)   Who had Ambrose refused to have in the house?
   (c)   What did Philip say to cousin Rachel when she told him how Ambrose had changed?
4 Philip's terrible jealousy returned. Who was Philip now jealous of?

10

1 How did Philip feel whenever cousin Rachel came into a room?
2 At the bank, Philip saw the collar of pearls.
   (a)   When did the brides of the Ashley family wear this collar?
   (b)   What did Philip tell the manager he was going to do with the pearls?
   (c)   What did the manager reply?
   (d)   What had Philip decided to do with the collar of pearls?
3 Nick Kendall told Philip: 'I have had some bad news from the bank.'
   (a)   What was the bad news?
   (b)   What did Philip say when he heard the news?
   (c)   What stories had Nick Kendall heard about Mrs Ashley and her first husband?

4 Nick Kendall said to Philip: 'If you do not ask Mrs Ashley to give
   back the collar of pearls, I will.'
   (a) Why did Nick Kendall have the right to ask for the collar
        of pearls to be returned to the bank?
   (b) What did Mrs Ashley do when she heard what Nick
        Kendall had said?
5 Philip told cousin Rachel that the Ashley brides wore the collar
   of pearls on their wedding-day. What wedding-day was Philip
   thinking of?

11

1 Philip was tired of Nick Kendall being his guardian.
   (a) When would Nick Kendall no longer be Philip's guardian?
   (b) What money could Philip spend until then?
   (c) What work had started in the gardens?
2 Philip found another letter from Ambrose in the pocket of an old coat.
   (a) Why had Ambrose not signed his new will?
   (b) What question did Ambrose ask Philip to answer for him?
   (c) What did Philip do with this letter?
3 That night, Philip asked cousin Rachel about Ambrose's new will.
   (a) What had Ambrose written in this new will?
   (b) What did cousin Rachel say were the reasons why Ambrose had
        not signed the new will?
4 Philip, with the help of a lawyer, wrote out a document.
   (a) What would happen in three weeks' time?
   (b) Would Mrs Ashley ever be able to sell the house or the land?
   (c) What would happen to the house and the land if Mrs
        Ashley married again or if she died?
5 How did Philip feel when Rainaldi was in the Ashley house?
6 What joke did Rainaldi make about the date of Philip's birthday?

12

1 On the last day of March, Philip showed Nick Kendall the
   document.
   (a) Why did Philip say he had written the document?
   (b) Why did Nick Kendall wish that Rainaldi had seen the document?
   (c) What question did Nick Kendall ask Philip?
   (d) How did Philip reply to this question?

2   What did Philip do as the clock was striking midnight on 31st March?
3   Philip stayed the night in Rachel's room. What did this make
     Philip believe about their relationship?
4   Why had cousin Rachel gone to see Nick Kendall?
5   Philip met cousin Rachel in the carriage when she was on her
     way back from Nick Kendall's house.
     (a)   What did Philip notice about Rachel's eyes when she lifted her veil?
     (b)   Why was Philip surprised when Rachel talked about Louise
           and about making plans to meet Louise in London?
6   Philip told the Kendalls: 'Rachel has promised to be my wife.'
     (a)   How did Rachel look when Philip said these words?
     (b)   What did Rachel say?
     (c)   Why had Rachel let Philip stay the night in her room?
7   Philip began to understand what Ambrose had suffered.
     (a)   What did Philip notice about Rachel's face?
     (b)   Who was now the owner of the Ashley house and estate?
     (c)   What did Philip do to frighten Rachel?

13

1   Philip said to Louise: 'But if Rachel marries me, she will lose nothing.'
     (a)   What had Nick Kendall said would happen if Rachel
           married again?
     (b)   What had Rachel said when she heard this?
     (c)   What did Louise say Mrs Ashley would not be able to do if
           she married Philip?
2   What happened to Philip when he was riding back home from his
     meeting with Louise?
3   Why did Rachel ask Mary Pascoe to stay in the Ashley house?
4   Philip asked cousin Rachel: 'Have you sent Mary Pascoe away?'
     (a)   How long had Philip been in bed ill?
     (b)   How had Philip been saved from death?
     (c)   What did Philip believe had happened on the day before
           his birthday?
5   As Philip got better, he was able to go out into the garden.
     (a)   What had the workmen been busy doing?
     (b)   What tree reminded Philip of his visit to Villa Sangalletti?
6   Seecombe told Philip that Mrs Ashley was going back to Florence.
     (a)   Why had Rachel not sold Villa Sangalletti?

(b)   Why did Philip think it was not right for Rachel to go to Italy for the winter?
(c)   What did Philip suddenly know?
(d)   What did Philip ask Rachel to do?

14

1   Why would Philip sometimes not think clearly?
2   Philip asked Rachel: 'Why is Rainaldi in the town?'
  (a)   What did Rachel reply?
  (b)   Why did Philip hate Rainaldi?
  (c)   What did Philip tell Rachel to do?
3   What was strange about the tisana Philip drank in the evenings?
4   That night, Philip searched Rachel's desk.
  (a)   What was Philip looking for?
  (b)   What did he find?
  (c)   What words that Ambrose had written did Philip remember?
5   What did the workman warn Philip about?
6   Why did Philip decide that he would never again drink anything Rachel gave him?
7   Philip said: 'You know now who killed Rachel.'
  (a)   How did Rachel die?
  (b)   Who killed her?
8   What do you think happened at Villa Sangalletti? Do you think Rachel poisoned Ambrose with the laburnum seeds?

GLOSSARY

Glossary

1 **guardian** (page 4)
someone who is responsible for a young person, his money and his property.

2 **gentleman of leisure** (page 4)
Ambrose was very rich. He did not have to work. He could spend his time doing what he liked.

3 **estate** (page 4)
Ambrose owned a large piece of land in the country, with many farms and fields and woods.

4 **shy** (page 4)
someone who is quiet and does not like to meet strangers.

5 **district** (page 4)
the part of the country where Ambrose's house was.

6 **expected** (page 5)
to think or believe that something will happen.

7 **judge** (page 6)
someone who decides if a person has done wrong or not.

8 **coach** (page 8)
a four-wheeled carriage pulled by four or six horses. In the 1830s coaches carried people from town to town.

9 **jealous** (page 9)
to be unhappy because someone you love, loves someone else.

10 **godfather** (page 10)
someone who promises to help parents look after a Christian child.

11 **disturbed** (page 11)
a person whose mind is disturbed is ill. He is unable to think clearly.

12 **tumour** (page 11)
something growing in the brain, which can cause madness and death.

13 **torment** (page 12)
Ambrose is saying that Rachel has made him feel great pain and unhappiness.

14 **funeral** (page 14)
putting a dead person into the ground.

15 **shuttered** (page 14)
the windows had wooden covers over them.

16 **courtyard** (page 14)
an unroofed space with walls or buildings around it.

17 **fountain** (page 14)
water pushed through pipes so that it rises in the air.
18 **laburnum tree** (page 14)
a small tree with long, yellow flowers. The seeds of the laburnum tree are poisonous. If a person eats them they can become ill and die.
19 **tisana** (page 14)
a drink made from herbs – the dried leaves of flowers and plants.
20 **terrace** (page 16)
a piece of ground on the side of a house, looking out onto the gardens.
21 **chest** (page 17)
a large box with a lid.
22 **warned** (page 18)
to tell someone that something bad or dangerous may happen.
23 **destroyed** (page 18)
to damage something so badly that it is useless.
24 **death certificate** (page 18)
a paper signed by a doctor which says how a person died.
25 **will** (page 18)
a paper written by a person which says what will happen to his property and money when he dies. The will must be signed by the person or it means nothing.
26 **suspected** (page 19)
Ambrose thought that Mrs Ashley was doing something wrong.
27 **dressed in black** (page 19)
at the time of this story, when a person died, his relatives, friends and servants wore black clothes. Black clothes were worn for a year after the death. This was called the period of mourning. The wife of the dead man was not able to marry for a year and did not wear brightly coloured clothes or jewellery.
28 **claim** (page 20)
to make a claim on a person's will (see Glossary no. 25 above) is to say that some of that person's money or property belongs to you.
29 **study** (page 20)
a room in a house where someone can work quietly and where business can be done.
30 **changed my mind** (page 21)
to change your mind is to decide to do something different.
31 **silver** (page 21)
candlesticks, plates, bowls, knives etc, made of silver.

32 **portrait** (page 21)
a painting of someone's face.
33 **awkwardly** (page 23)
when Philip met Rachel for the first time he felt very
uncomfortable. He did not know what to say or what to do.
Because of this he spoke awkwardly.
34 **longing** (page 23)
wanting to do something very much.
35 **hesitated** (page 23)
to start saying a word and then to stop because you are not sure
what you want to say.
36 **tea** – *tea is served* (page 25)
at the time of this story tea was the drink usually taken after the
evening meal.
37 **hard** (page 25)
unkind
38 **remind** (page 25)
Philip looked very much like Ambrose. When Rachel looked at
him she remembered Ambrose.
39 **shawl** (page 26)
a cloth worn over the head and shoulders by women.
40 **sewing** (page 27)
working with a needle and coloured threads onto cloth.
41 **accuse** (page 28)
to accuse someone is to say that they have done something
wrong. Philip believed that Rachel had been very unkind to
Ambrose and had made him suffer such great pain and
unhappiness that he had died. Now Philip wanted to make
Rachel suffer in the same way.
42 **spoilt** (page 30)
someone who has always been given what they wanted.
43 **entertaining** (page 31)
inviting guests and giving them meals in your house.
44 **widow** (page 31)
a woman whose husband has died.
45 **quarter** (page 33)
every quarter is every three months.
46 **generous** (page 33)
to give someone presents and money.
47 **impulsive** (page 33)
deciding to do something quickly and without thinking.

48 **ashamed** (page 34)
feeling that you have done something wrong or foolish.
49 **tenants** (page 36)
farmers and workers on the estate.
50 **herbs** (page 36)
see Glossary no. 19–*tisana*.
51 **mourning clothes** (page 40)
see Glossary no. 27–dressed in black.
52 **collar of pearls** (page 40)
a string of small, white stones worn round the neck.
53 **bride** (page 40)
a woman who is to be married.
54 **decorated** (page 40)
in Europe, at Christmas time, many people bring a green tree into
the house. The tree is decorated with coloured paper and lights.
People give each other presents that have been put on the tree.
55 **overdrawn** (page 42)
Mrs Ashley was spending more money than she had in the bank.
56 **sunken water-garden** (page 43)
a garden which has many steps leading down to it. It is decorated
with pools, fountains (see Glossary no. 17), trees and plants.
57 **violent** (page 44)
wanting to fight and hit people.
58 **All Fools' Day** (page 47)
1st April. On the morning of 1st April, people in England play
tricks on one another and do foolish things.
59 **veil** (page 50)
a very thin piece of cloth worn over a woman's face.
60 **forgive** (page 52)
to excuse someone when he has done something wrong.
61 **apologize** (page 52)
to say you are sorry when you have done something wrong.
62 **deceived** (page 53)
tricked someone, told them lies.
63 **inn** (page 57)
a place where people stay for the night and have drinks and

Exercises

Background

Complete the gaps. Use each word or phrase in the box once.

> health   refused   look after   alone   same   ~~died~~   grew up
> twenty   always   brother   suggested   married   house
> garden   sudden   neither   cousin   knowledge   Rachel
> property   impulsive   age   surprise   enough   hard

My parents [1] *died* when I was young and I [2] ....
with my cousin Ambrose. He was [3] .... years my
senior, but I [4] .... thought of him as a
[5] ....

Ambrose was not [6] .... He had a large
[7] .... with gardens and a park, but he had
[8] .... wife nor child. He made a will and left
all his [9] .... to me.

At the [10] .... of forty, Ambrose began to look old. The
English winter was too [11] .... for him. His doctor
[12] .... that he move to Italy. Perhaps his
[13] .... would improve in a warmer country.

I wanted to go with him to Florence. Ambrose was kind, but he
[14] .... 'Who will [15] ....
the house?' he asked. 'You are old [16] .... to
take care of the Ashley estate. Soon it will all be yours.'

80

He wrote to me from Florence. Somehow he had met my distant

17.. Rachel. She lived in a villa with a fine

18...................................... and she had a great 19..

of plants and medicines. Ambrose loved gardens too. Rachel's husband

was dead and she was 20... in the world. To my

21............................., Ambrose wrote to say that he and

22.. were married. It seemed very

23.., but Ambrose was an

24.. man – and I am the

25.. .

Word Focus 1: *suggest*

Rewrite the sentences using the verb *suggest*.

1   The doctor said to Ambrose, 'You should move to Italy.'
    The doctor suggested that he move to Italy.
    ....

2   Mr Kendall said to Philip, 'You should go to Florence.'
    ....

3   Signor Rainaldi said to Rachel, 'You should buy the Villa Sangalletti.'
    ....

4   Rachel said to Philip, 'You should get married.'
    ....

5   Rachel said to Philip, 'You should drink tisana.'
    ....

6   Rachel said to Philip, 'You should build a sunken garden.'
    ....

7   Rachel said to Philip, 'You should take some medicine.'

    ....

8   Rachel said to Ambrose, 'You should make a new will.'

    ....

Grammar Focus 1: Past Continuous Passive

Rewrite the sentences using the Past Continuous Passive.

1   Ambrose thought that someone was poisoning him.
    Ambrose thought that he was being poisoned.
    ....

2   Ambrose thought that someone was deceiving him.

    ....

3   Ambrose thought that someone was taking his money.

    ....

4   Ambrose thought that someone was reading his letters.

    ....

5   Ambrose thought that someone was hiding his clothes.

    ....

6   Ambrose thought that someone was watching him.

    ....

7   Ambrose thought that someone was lying to him.

    ....

8   Ambrose thought that someone was overdrawing his account.

    ....
    ....

Making Sentences

Write questions for the answers.

1 *Who was put in charge of the estate in Philip's absence?*
   The head servant was put in charge of the estate in Philip's absence.

2 *How*
   Ambrose had been dead for three weeks.

3 *What*
   Ambrose had not signed his new will.

4 *Who*
   Mr Kendall had been made guardian of the estate.

5 *When*
   Philip would inherit the Ashley estate when he was twenty-five.

6 *How*
   Philip could draw money from his account by applying to Mr Kendall.

7 *Why*
   He did not wish to see his cousin Rachel because he believed that she had poisoned Ambrose.

8 *How much*

   Rachel had received nothing from her husband's will.

9 *What*
   Rachel would have to give Italian lessons to earn a living.

10 *Why*
   Philip changed his mind about Rachel because he fell in love with her.

Grammar Focus 2: conditional sentences

Write conditional sentences to describe what might have happened.

1 Ambrose did not change his will. Philip received everything.
If Ambrose had changed his will, Philip would not have received everything.

2 Philip did not arrive in time. Ambrose died.

3 Rachel did not stay in the villa. Philip suspected her.

4 Rachel was careless with money. Ambrose did not leave his estate to her.

5 Philip did not listen to Mr Kendall. He took the pearls from the bank.

6 Philip did not marry Louise. He was unhappy.

7 Philip was not experienced. He gave everything to Rachel.

8 Philip did not tell Rachel about the unfinished bridge. She died.

Words From The Story

Unjumble the letters to find words from the story, and complete the sentences.

1 **diwow**   Rachel's husband was dead.

   She was a ....widow................ .

2 **asette**   Ambrose Ashley owned a large house with a park and gardens.

   He had a large ....

3 **ridbusted**   Ambrose was not only sick in his body, he was also sick in his mind.

   His mind was ....

4 **antisa**   Rachel made a kind of tea from herbs and seeds.

   She made ....

5 **lunafer**   Rachel went away from Florence after Ambrose was buried.

   She left after the ....

6 **santifoun**   The garden had many pools with jets of water.

   It had many ....

7 **irmended**   Philip looked like Ambrose.

   He .... Rachel of her husband.

8 **warndover**   Rachel took out more money than was in her account.

   Her account was ....

9 **roguenes**   'You give too much money away,' said Mr Kendall.

   He thought Philip was too ....'

10	**silumpive**	'You act too quickly. You act without thinking,' said Mr Kendall.
		He thought Philip was too ....'
11	**soniopous**	The seeds of the laburnum are green and deadly.
		They are ....
12	**viedeced**	'She has not told you the truth. She has written letters behind your back,' said Louise.
		She thought Rachel had .... Philip.

Word Focus 2: *accuse*

Rewrite the sentences using the verb *accuse*.

1 Ambrose said he was being poisoned and that Rachel was responsible.
Ambrose accused Rachel of poisoning him.
....

2 Ambrose said his bank account was empty and that Rachel was to blame.

....

....

3 Ambrose said his will had been altered and that Rainaldi did it.

....

....

4 Ambrose said he was given bad food and that it was the servants' fault.

....

....

5 Ambrose said that Rachel was in love with Rainaldi.

....

....

Multiple Choice

Tick the best answer.

1 Rachel was in mourning for Ambrose. What does this mean?
a ☐ She was waiting for him before midday.
b ☑ She was wearing black clothes in remembrance.
c ☐ She was waiting to inherit the estate.

2 What document did Signor Rainaldi send to Mr Kendall?
a ☐ A letter from the bank saying that the account was overdrawn.
b ☐ Ambrose's second will that left everything to Rachel.
c ☐ A certificate signed by a doctor stating that Ambrose had died naturally.

3 Philip inherited the Ashley estate. Ambrose had made Philip his ....
a ☐ heir.
b ☐ guardian.
c ☐ trustee.

4 Why did Ambrose not want Philip to inherit the estate until he was twenty-five years old?
a ☐ Because Ambrose was twenty years older than Philip.
b ☐ He thought that Philip was still young and inexperienced.
c ☐ A man could not vote until he was twenty-five years old in 1838.

5 Why did Philip want to marry Rachel?
a ☐ He wanted her to have the estate.
b ☐ Ambrose had left her nothing.
c ☐ He was in love with her.

6 What had made Philip ill?
a ☐ His broken heart.
b ☐ A brain tumour.
c ☐ Laburnum seeds.

Published by Macmillan Heinemann ELT
Between Towns Road, Oxford OX4 3PP
Macmillan Heinemann ELT is an imprint of
Macmillan Publishers Limited
Companies and representatives throughout the world
Heinemann is a registered trademark of Pearson Education, used under licence.

ISBN 978 0 2300 3531 7
ISBN 978 1 4050 7715 6 (with CD pack)

This retold version by Margaret Tarner for Macmillan Readers
First published 1980
Text © Macmillan Publishers Limited 2002, 2005
Design and illustration © Macmillan Publishers Limited 2002, 2005

This edition first published 2005

Illustrated by Kay Dixey
Original cover template design by Jackie Hill
Cover photography by Corbis/PBNJ

Printed in Thailand
2010 2009 2008
5 4 3 2 1

with CD pack
2015 2014 2013
13 12 11 10